Howard B. Wigglebottom
Learns It's OK to Back Away

Howard Binkow

Susan F. Cornelison

Written by: Howard Binkow
Illustrated by: Susan F. Cornelison
Book design by: Tobi S. Cunningham

Thunderbolt Publishing
We Do Listen Foundation
www.wedolisten.com

This book is the result of a joint creative effort with Ana Rowe and Susan F. Cornelison.

Gratitude and appreciation are given to all those who reviewed the story prior to publication.
The book became much better by incorporating several of their suggestions.

Karen Binkow, Committee for Children, Sandra Duckworth, Lillian Freeman, LCSW,
Sherry Holland, Renee Keeler, Lori Kotarba, Tracy Mastalski, Gary Norcross, Teri Poulus, Chris Primm, Laurie Sachs, Anne Shacklett, Mimi
C. Savio, C.J. Shuffler, Nancey Silvers, Gayle Smith, Joan Sullivan, Carrie Sutton, Rosemary Underwood, and George Sachs Walor.

Teachers, librarians, counselors, and students at:

Alcott Elementary, Westerville, Ohio
Bossier Parish Schools, Bossier City, Louisiana
Central Elementary, Beaver Falls, Pennsylvania
Chalker Elementary, Kennesaw, Georgia
Charleston Elementary, Charleston, Arkansas
Glen Alpine Elementary, Morganton, North Carolina
Golden West Elementary, Manteca, California
Iveland Elementary School, St. Louis, Missouri

Kincaid Elementary, Marietta, Georgia
Lee Elementary, Los Alamitos, California
Meadows Elementary, Manhattan Beach, California
Prestonwood Elementary, Dallas, Texas
Sherman Oaks Elementary, Sherman Oaks, California
Walt Disney Magnet School, Chicago, Illinois
West Navarre Primary, Navarre, Florida
Washington-Franklin Elementary School, Farmington, Missouri

Printed in the U.S.A.

First printing June 2010

ISBN 978-0-9715390-9-9

This book belongs to

_____

I'm Howard B. Wigglebottom.
I want to be the Ninja Bunny.

I have to take a time-out all day.
Everybody has been saying I do the
wrong things when I get angry.

Well, that makes me
MAD!

. . . and sad, too." Howard had time to think about his day because he wasn't allowed to go outside and play.

He remembered being really happy at the beginning of the day. Lunch was spaghetti and meatballs. To top it off, it was chocolate milk Wednesday. He couldn't wait.

His stomach was making funny noises. Howard wasn't thinking about schoolwork because he kept looking at the clock, waiting for lunchtime.

9

FINALLY, the bell rang and everyone lined up to go to the lunchroom. Howard was so excited he cut right to the front of the line. **"HEY, HE CUT!"** his friends complained.

"Did you cut in line?" asked the lunch lady.
"Please go to the end."

HOWARD DID NOT GET HIS WAY.

He kept his eyes on the
chocolate milk.

"OH NO!"

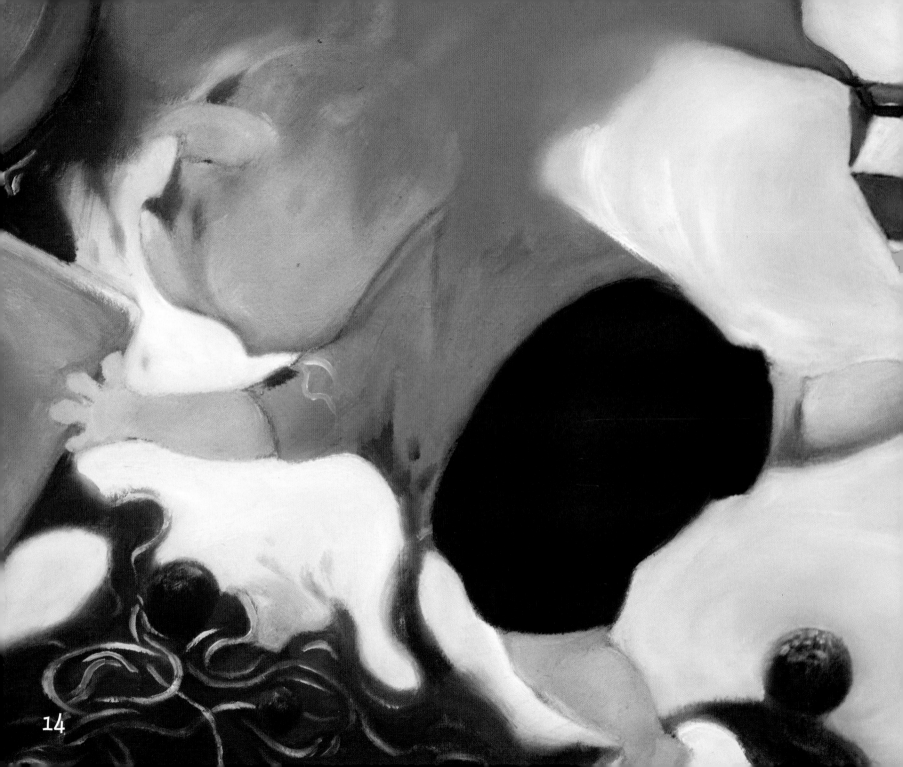

14

A A A A Y Y Y I E E E

There wasn't enough, and Bob reached for the last one!

Howard knew what he had to do!

"THAT'S MY CHOCOLATE MILK!" cried Howard. He
tried to kick the milk out of Bob's hands the Ninja way. He
went flying through the air. So did Bob, the spaghetti, meatballs,
AND the last carton of chocolate milk.

HOWARD DID NOT GET HIS WAY.

"What a mess you made, Howard. Clean that up at once!"
said the lunch lady.

While everyone else was eating Howard's favorite lunch, he
was mopping the floor. He was hungry and very grumpy when
Bob walked by and said, "Hey, you missed a spot!"

Howard got a strange feeling in his tummy. His heart started pounding really fast and his hands made a tight fist. Then he saw **RED.**

Howard B. Wigglebottom, Ninja Bunny wannabe, TOTALLY LOST HIS COOL! He jumped toward Bob but missed and fell right into the mess.

HOWARD DID NOT GET HIS WAY.

"That's IT, Howard B. Wigglebottom," said the lunch lady.
"I'm taking YOU to the principal."

After school, thinking about his day made Howard very sad. His mom interrupted his thoughts. "Howard, your friend Ali is here."

"I'm sorry you can't come out and play," said Ali.

"Me too," said Howard. "How come you don't have time-outs? Don't you ever get angry?"

"Well, I do," said Ali. "Just like everyone else."

"When I don't get my way, my tummy feels all tight. Before I do the wrong thing, I say . . . 'Stop; it's OK to back away.' Then I go out and do something to feel good again."

"Will you show me how?" asked Howard.

"Sure. When I really listen to my tummy," said Ali, "it lets me know if I'm scared, hungry, or angry. If it's tight, I'm pretty sure I'm angry."

Every day after school, Ali helped Howard listen to his tummy, back away, and do things to feel good . . .

25

throwing a ball

kicking a ball

After a few weeks of practice, Howard hardly ever lost his cool. He learned that when he doesn't get his way, he says . . . "Stop; that's OK." He listens to his tummy, backs away, and then goes out to play.

28

Howard B. Wigglebottom Learns It's OK to Back Away
Suggestions for Lessons and Reflections

★ **WHAT IS ANGER?**

Anger is a strong, bad feeling we have for a person or thing. We all get angry.

What makes your friend angry might not make you angry. Some of us get very angry, others just a little. Some of us can get very angry very fast. Others get angry slowly.

Different things make us angry at different times. When we feel hungry and tired we are more likely to get angry.

Usually when we feel angry we feel the need to hurt the person or the thing that is angering us. We might do things that will get us in trouble (like using bad words, hitting, kicking, etc.) and later on feel really sorry about it.

To stop feeling bad about ourselves and getting in trouble, it's important to find out what makes us angry and how to stop doing the wrong things. Remember, we never want to hurt or get hurt.

★ **WHAT MAKES US ANGRY? WHAT DO WE LOOK LIKE, AND WHAT DO WE DO?**

Most of us will feel angry when we can't get our way; that means when we can't get what we want fast. We also usually feel angry when someone tells lies about us, breaks our things, or takes them without permission.

Can you tell what makes your friends, teachers and loved ones angry? How about on TV shows and cartoons? What do they look like when they are angry? Can you tell which of these faces look sad, scared or angry?

What do the people you know say when they get angry? What made Howard angry in the book and what did he do when he got angry? Howard got angry when he couldn't get what he wanted, and then he did the wrong things. Do you know what makes you angry? Do you always want to be first? Do you like to share your things? Do you feel angry when you can't get what you want? What do you do when you are angry? Ask the people at home and at school to tell you what they think will make you angry and what you do when you get angry.

★ **LISTENING TO OUR TUMMY**

When we feel good and happy our bodies feel nice and strong. When we feel angry, scared, or sad our bodies don't feel good.

When we are not sure about how we feel, we can find out quickly just by paying attention to our bodies. Our hearts will beat faster or slower, we might feel hot or cold, our faces can get reddish or very white, and our tummies may feel tight or shaky or upset. The easiest part of the body for us to pay attention to is the tummy. It will take a lot of practice to get good at it.

Start by paying attention to your tummy when you are feeling good. Touch your belly, feel the skin, move and shake your belly around. Notice how it moves nicely. Then, listen to your tummy when it's hungry. Most of us feel a little upset when we are hungry and our tummies make noises. When we touch it and move it around, it does not feel so nice. If we practice listening to our tummies every day, they will let us know when we are angry, sad, and scared, too. We will notice how it does not feel good at all. Remember: It takes practice to be good at it!

★ IT'S OK TO BACK AWAY

Whenever we feel our tummy is tight and we are feeling angry, we have to back away–right away–before we do the wrong things. Say "Stop. It is OK to back away"–then walk away.

When you can't walk away, stand on one foot, then the other, and keep changing your feet.

No one is good at doing this the first time. It takes a lot of practice. Think about how many hours the champions practice every day!

★ THINGS TO DO TO FEEL GOOD AGAIN

When we back away before doing the wrong things, we will feel very nice. But it will take a while for our bodies to catch up and feel good again. The fastest way to make our bodies feel good again is to go outside and play. Do things that our bodies like to do: run, jump, kick, throw a ball, clap fast and hard, spin around, or scream "Ninja Bunny!" (or anything you like) three times.

If it's not possible to go outside: Count your fingers and toes forward and back ten times. Look at a pet, a tree, or a flower while you count to one hundred. Think of a person you like, someone you said "thank you" to, or someone who was very nice to you. Interlace your fingers one way then another several times. Slap your tummy gently five times, rest, then slap it again; do it many times. Tell someone how you feel. Sing a song that you like. Try to whistle, or draw a picture in colors about a place you would like to go.

PLEASE CONTACT US AT WEDOLISTEN.COM AND SHARE YOUR WAYS TO BACK AWAY AND TO FEEL GOOD AGAIN.

Learn more about Howard's other adventures.

BOOKS

Howard B. Wigglebottom Learns to Listen
Howard B. Wigglebottom Listens to His Heart
Howard B. Wigglebottom Learns About Bullies
Howard B. Wigglebottom Learns About Mud and Rainbows
Howard B. Labougeotte apprend à ècouter

WEBSITE

www.wedolisten.com

Free animated books, educational games, and activities, resources, songs,
lessons, posters, and e-cards.

You may e-mail the author at howardb@wedolisten.com.

Comments and suggestions are appreciated.